NO. C.D.

ONE WEEK LOAN

The Art and Science
of Digital Compositing

Limited Warranty and Disclaimer of Liability

Academic Press ("AP") and anyone else who has been involved in the creation or production of the accompanying code ("the product") cannot and do not warrant the performance or results that may be obtained by using the product. The product is sold "as is" without warranty of any kind (except as hereafter described), either expressed or implied, including, but not limited to, any warranty of performance or any implied warranty of merchantability or fitness for any particular purpose. AP warrants only that the magnetic diskette(s) on which the code is recorded is free from defects in material and faulty workmanship under the normal use and service for a period of ninety (90) days from the date the product is delivered. The purchaser's sole and exclusive remedy in the event of a defect is expressly limited to either replacement of the diskette(s) or refund of the purchase price, at AP's sole discretion.

In no event, whether as a result of breach of contract, warranty or tort (including negligence), will AP or anyone who has been involved in the creation or production of the product be liable to purchaser for any damages, including any lost profits, lost savings or other incidental or consequential damages arising out of the use or inability to use the product or any modifications thereof, or due to the contents of the code, even if AP has been advised of the possibility of such damages, or for any claim by any other party.

Any request for replacement of a defective diskette must be postage prepaid and must be accompanied by the original defective diskette, your mailing address and telephone number, and proof of date of purchase and purchase price. Send such requests, stating the nature of the problem, to Academic Press Customer Service, 6277 Sea Harbor Drive, Orlando, FL 32887, 1-800-321-5068. AP shall have no obligation to refund the purchase price or to replace a diskette based on claims of defects in the nature or operation of the product.

Some states do not allow limitation on how long an implied warranty lasts, nor exclusions or limitations of incidental or consequential damage, so the above limitations and exclusions may not apply to you. This warranty gives you specific legal rights, and you may also have other rights which vary from jurisdiction to jurisdiction.

The re-export of United States origin software is subject to the United States laws under the Export Administration Act of 1969 as amended. Any further sale of the product shall be in compliance with the United States Department of Commerce Administration Regulations. Compliance with such regulations is your responsibility and not the responsibility of AP.

The Art and Science of Digital Compositing

Ron Brinkmann

Morgan Kaufmann

An Imprint of Elsevier

Cover image: "The Two Ways of Life" by Oscar Gustav Rejlander. Image courtesy of The Royal Photographic Society Collection, Bath, England. Web site http://www.rps.org.

This book is printed on acid-free paper. ∞

ACADEMIC PRESS
An Imprint of Elsevier
525 B Street, Suite 1900, San Diego, CA 92101-4495 USA
http://www.academicpress.com

ACADEMIC PRESS
24-28 Oval Road, London NW1 7DX United Kingdom
http://www.hbuk.co.uk/ap/

MORGAN KAUFMANN
An Imprint of Elsevier
340 Pine Street, 6th Floor, San Francisco, CA 94104-3205 USA
http://www.mkp.com

Library of Congress Catalog Number: 99-60086
ISBN-13: 978-0-12-133960-9   ISBN-10: 0-12-133960-2

Printed in the United States of America
05 06 07 08 IP 9 8 7

For Mom and Dad,
of course.

Contents

Acknowledgments

This book would never have been completed without the help of a number of different people. Many of these people are listed here, but many, many others who gave me ideas, information, and inspiration are not, primarily due to the fallibility of my memory. To them I apologize, and hope that the fact that their wisdom is being propagated and utilized is at least some small consolation.

Thanks, first of all, to Tom Stone, whose enthusiasm for this book convinced me that it was worth doing, and who was the only publisher I talked to who understood why I was asking for so many of those expensive color plates! Thanks also to Tom's colleagues, Thomas Park and Julie Champagne, who hand-held me throughout the process.

Several different companies contributed the images that are discussed in Chapter 16. Specifically, Centropolis Effects in Santa Monica, CA (*Independence Day*), Digital Domain in Venice, CA (*Titanic* and the Budweiser "Lizards" commercial), Dreamquest Images in Simi Valley, CA (*Con Air*), Dreamworks SKG in Burbank, CA (*The Prince of Egypt*), Sony Pictures Imageworks in Culver City, CA (*James and the Giant Peach* and *Speed*), and VIFX in Marina Del Rey, CA (*T-Rex: Back to the Cretaceous*, *X-Files: Fight the Future*, and *Star Trek: Insurrection*). The following people were interviewed about the creation of the specific shots that are discussed: Jean-Luc Azzis for the Budweiser commercial, Jonathan Egstad for *Titanic*, Conny Fauser for *Independence Day*, Richard Hollander for *T-Rex*, David Morehead for *The Prince of Egypt*, Marlo Pabon for *Con Air*, Mark Rodahl for *Star Trek*, and John Wash for *X-Files*.

A number of other people helped with the book during its development, from the original SIGGRAPH course notes to the final proofreading. Thanks to Jerome Chen, Gary Jackemuk, Ashley Beck, Jeanette Volturno, Amy Wixson, Charlie Clavedetcher, Buckley Collum, John Carey, and Michelle Steinau, for their input, feedback, and support. Thanks to Mike Wassel at Illusion Arts for his help in photographing many of the example images that are used throughout the book.

Thanks to Alex, Aundrea, Alyssa, Rachel, Anna, and Josh, because I would be a poor uncle indeed if I passed up the opportunity for them to see their names in print, and thanks to Mandy and Ace (Plate 28).

A special note of thanks to my associates at Nothing Real, not only for the use of their fine compositing software to create many of the images in this book, but also for the assistance, encouragement, and knowledge of everyone there: Dan Candela, Louis Cetorelli, Allen Edwards, Arnaud and Fleur Hervas, Sid Joyner, Emmanuel Mogenet, and Peter Warner.

Finally, and above all, I have to thank all the digital compositing artists that I have had the pleasure of working with over the years, as well as the rest of the incredibly creative people in this industry who produce the fantastic images that feed and fill our imaginations. Keep up the excellent work.

Preface

This book is about creating images. It will discuss a number of different tools that can be used to create these images, but it is not a book about tools. In the years that I have been involved with the field of digital compositing, there have been dramatic increases in the power and flexibility of the tools that are available. But the basic concepts have remained the same, and this will most likely continue to be the case for the foreseeable future. Consequently, this book is not intended to be about how to use any specific piece of software—there are too many different tools, and they are changing too quickly. Rather, it is intended to give the reader the information that he or she needs in order to sit down in front of any piece of digital compositing software and be productive. Having been through the process of hiring quite a few compositing artists for the films on which I've worked, I almost always base my choice on the candidate's general compositing experience and not on whether they know how to use a specific package. Knowing where the buttons are located isn't nearly as important as knowing why to press those buttons.

The scope of techniques that fall under the category of digital compositing is actually quite large, from simple wire removals to assembling complex scenes with hundreds of disparate elements. The tools can range in cost from hundreds of thousands of dollars at the high end down to virtually nothing (shareware) at the low end. A person may spend only a few hours on a simple shot, or teams of people may spend months on a complex shot. Every shot is new; every shot is different. That's what makes the field so challenging, and it's also why no book can ever hope to be the final word on the subject.

My primary guideline for myself was to write the book that I wish someone had handed me when I first got started in this business. Although there is certainly no substitute for working alongside experienced professionals, I hope this book will be a good starting place for those new to the field. At the same time, I wanted it to be something that people who have been in the business for a while will also find useful. Straddling the fence can be a somewhat uncomfortable position at times, but I hope the compromise proves worthwhile.

Please feel free to send me feedback on the book, including any specific suggestions for improvements and corrections. I can be reached through my publisher, or e-mail me directly at rbrinkmann@nothingreal.com. I can't promise that I'll be able to reply to everyone, but I will read whatever you send.

The Art and Science
of Digital Compositing

CHAPTER ONE

Introduction to Digital Compositing

A massive spacecraft hovers over New York, throwing the entire city into shadow. A pair of lizards, sitting in the middle of a swamp, discuss their favorite beer. Dinosaurs, long extinct, live and breathe again, and the Titanic, submerged for decades, sails once more.

Usually the credit for these fantastic visuals is given to "CGI" (computer-generated imagery) or "computer graphics," an attribution that not only broadly simplifies the technology used, but also ignores the sizeable crew of talented artists who actually created the work. Computer graphics techniques, in conjunction with a myriad of other disciplines, *are* commonly used for the creation of visual effects in feature films. But the term "computer graphics" is broad and covers a wide variety of methods that rely on a computer to help produce images. Many of these methods are merely traditional methods that have been updated to take advantage of modern tools. In fact, even the typesetting of a book like this is now almost completely done using a computer, and as such this page could loosely be considered a piece of "computer graphics."

When dealing with computer graphics as used for the creation and manipulation of images, we will usually break the subject down into two primary subcategories: **3D graphics**[1] and **2D graphics.** The names indicate whether the work is

---

[1] Do not confuse 3D imagery with stereoscopic imagery, a topic that we will discuss in Chapter 12.

considered primarily three-dimensional in nature, or two-dimensional. The first category, the "3D" work, involves creating a complete model of an object within the computer. This model can be viewed from any angle, can be positioned relative to an imaginary camera, and can generally be manipulated as if it were a real object, yet it exists only within the computer. Even though the way we are interacting with the object is still based on a two-dimensional display device (the computer's monitor), the model itself is a mathematical simulation of a true three-dimensional object. This model can be lit, textured, and given the ability to move and change. Once a particular camera view is chosen and the color, lighting, and animation are acceptable, special software will **render** the scene to produce a sequence of images.

While the 3D aspect of visual effects seems to get a great deal of recognition, it is only one piece of the puzzle that makes up a finished shot. The other half of the visual effects process involves working with preexisting images, manipulating and combining them to produce new images. These images can be from just about any source, including rendered images produced by the 3D process. This process of manipulating existing images is identified as being "2D" work because of the flat, two-dimensional images with which it deals and because there is essentially no attempt to introduce any three-dimensional data into the process. Not every film that makes use of visual effects will include 3D work, but any time there is a visual effect in a film, you can assume that 2D work was done. It is the backbone of visual effects work, and the final, most important step in the creation of the desired imagery.

Even with a fully 3D movie such as Pixar's *Toy Story*, 2D effects and tools are used to enhance and integrate the rendered 3D images. 2D manipulations have historically been accomplished via a number of different methods, as we'll discuss in a moment. But these days, most 2D work is done with the aid of computers, and the bulk of this 2D work is classified as digital compositing.

DEFINITION

Digital compositing, as we are going to be discussing it, deals with the process of integrating images from multiple sources into a single, seamless whole. While many of these techniques apply to still images, we will be looking at tools and methods that are useful and reasonable for large **sequences** of images as well. Before we go any further, let's come up with a specific definition for what this book is all about.

Digital Compositing: The digitally manipulated combination of at least two source images to produce an integrated result.

By far the most difficult part of this digital compositing process is producing the integrated result—an image that doesn't betray that its creation was owed to multiple source elements. In particular, we are usually attempting to produce (sequences of) images that could have been believably photographed without the use of any postprocessing. Colloquially, they should look "real." Even if the elements in the scene are obviously *not* real (huge talking insects standing atop a giant peach, for example), one must be able to believe that everything in the scene was photographed at the same time, by the same camera.

Although so far we've mentioned only a few big-budget examples of digital compositing being put to use, in reality you'll find digital compositing at work just about anywhere you look in today's world of media and advertising. Pull a magazine off the shelf and in all likelihood you will find that most of the art and graphics have been put together using some sort of computerized paint program. Television commercials are more likely than not to have been composited together from multiple sources. Yet whether the digital compositing process is used for a business presentation or for feature-film special effects, the techniques and tools employed all follow the same basic principles.

This book is intended to be an overview that will be useful to *anyone* who uses digital compositing. However, you will probably notice that many topics, descriptions, and examples seem to approach the subject from the perspective of someone working to produce visual effects for feature films. This emphasis is not only due to the author's experience in this field, but also because feature-film work tends to push the limits of the process in terms of techniques, technology, and budgets. Consequently, it is an ideal framework to use in providing an overview of the subject. Additionally, it allows for the use of examples and sample images that are already familiar to most readers.

The title of this book, *The Art and Science of Digital Compositing,* was coined to stress the fact that true mastery of digital compositing includes both technical and artistic skills. As with any art form, the artist must certainly have a good amount of technical proficiency with the tools that will be used. These tools could potentially include any number of different hardware and software compositing systems. But one should also become knowledgeable about the science of the *entire* compositing process, not just specific tools. This would include everything from an understanding of the way that visual data is represented in a digital format to knowledge of how a camera reacts to light and color. Please remember, though, that all these technical considerations are simply factors to weigh when confronted with the question of "Does it *look* right?" The answer will ultimately be a subjective judgment, and a good compositor who is able to consistently make the decisions that produce quality images will always be in high demand.

The combination of multiple sources to produce a new image is certainly nothing new, and was being done long before computers entered the picture (pardon the pun). Although this book is about *digital* compositing, let's spend a moment looking at the foundations upon which digital compositing is built.

HISTORICAL PERSPECTIVE

In the summer of 1857, the Swedish-born photographer Oscar G. Rejlander set out to create what would prove to be the most technically complicated photograph that had ever been produced. Working at his studio in England, Rejlander selectively combined the imagery from 32 different glass negatives to produce a single, massive print. A reproduction of this print, which was titled *The Two Ways of Life*, is shown in Figure 1.1. It is one of the earliest examples of what came to be known as a "combination print."

Had the artist wished to capture this image on a single negative, he would have required a huge studio and many models. Even then, it is doubtful whether he could have lit the scene with as much precision or have positioned all the people in exactly the fashion he desired. Certainly it could have proven to be an expensive, time-consuming process. Instead, he painstakingly shot small groups of people and sets, adjusting each for the position and size that he would need them to be. In some cases, the only way to make them small enough in frame was to photograph them reflected in a mirror. Once the various negatives were created, the combination process involved selectively uncovering only a portion of the printing paper and exposing the desired negative to that area.

The scene that resulted from this complex undertaking was designed to depict the two paths that one may choose in life. The right side of the image represents the righteous path, with individual figures who illustrate Religion, Knowledge, Mercy, Married Life, and so on. The left side of the image depicts somewhat less lofty goals, with figures representing everything from Idleness to Gambling to Licentiousness to Murder. Photography was only just becoming accepted as a true art form, but Rejlander's work was immediately recognized as an attempt at something more than the typical documentary or narrative photographs of the time. This is important to understand, since it points out that Rejlander used this combination technique in pursuit of a specific vision, *not* as a gimmick. There was a great deal of science involved, but more important, a great deal of art.

While *The Two Ways of Life* received quite a bit of recognition, it was also the subject of some controversy. Although part of this had to do with its subject matter (a Scottish exhibition of the work actually hung a drape over the nudity-rich left half of the image), the issue of whether or not such "trick" photography was ethical or artistically valid was continually raised. Eventually Rejlander himself denounced the practice, stating

Figure 1.1   *An early composite photograph, Oscar Gustav Rejlander's The Two Ways of Life. (Photo courtesy of The Royal Photographic Society Collection, Bath, England. Web site http://www.rps.org)*

> I am tired of photography for the public—particularly composite
> photographs, for there *can be no gain,* and there is no honour, but
> cavil and misinterpretation.

Fortunately, the techniques continued to be used and refined even without Rejlander's support, and few people today consider compositing (at least conceptually)
to be particularly dishonorable.

Motion picture photography came about in the late 1800s, and the desire to be
able to continue this sort of image combination drove the development of specialized hardware to expedite the process. **Optical printers** were built that could
selectively combine multiple pieces of film, and **optical compositing** was born.
Optical compositing is still a valid and often-used process. Many of the techniques
and skills developed by optical compositors are directly applicable to the digital
realm, and in many cases, certain digital tools can trace not only their conceptual
origin but also their basic algorithms directly to optical methodologies. Consequently, the digital compositing artist would be well served by researching the
optical compositing process in addition to seeking out information on digital
methods.

A number of early examples of optical compositing can be found in the 1933
film *King Kong.* The image shown in Figure 1.2 is actually a composite image that
was created in the following fashion: The giant ape was photographed first—a
16-inch tall miniature that was animated using **stop-motion** techniques. This
process involves photographing the model one frame at a time, changing the pose
or position of the character between each frame. The result, when played back at
normal speed, is a continuously animating object. After this footage was developed
and processed, it was projected onto a large **rear projection** screen that was
positioned on a full-sized stage. The foreground action (the actress in the tree)
was then photographed while the background footage was being projected behind
it, producing a composite image. This particular type of compositing is known
as an **in-camera effect**, since there was no additional post-production work needed
to complete the shot. Other scenes in the film were accomplished using an early
form of **bluescreen** photography (which we will discuss further in Chapters 5
and 13), where the foreground and background were photographed separately
and then later combined in an optical printing step.

Nowadays, optical compositing equipment has been largely (but not completely) replaced with general-purpose computer systems and some highly specialized software, but the concepts have not really changed. Before we start our
discussion of these software tools, let's take a look at an example of one of these
digital composites. We won't go into a great deal of detail about this particular
example just yet, but will initially use it to start presenting some of the common
terminology used throughout the industry, as well as throughout this book.

Figure 1.2 *An early motion-picture composite, from the film* King Kong. *(KING KONG © 1933 Turner Entertainment Co.)*

TERMINOLOGY

The example that we'll be dealing with is a scene from the feature film *James and the Giant Peach*, and is shown in Plate 1. This particular composite was created from a multitude of different original images. We usually refer to the individual pieces from which we create our final composite as **elements**. Elements in this composite include the following:

- The giant peach, shown as a separate element in Plate 2a. The peach is a miniature element, about a foot in diameter, and was photographed on a stage in front of a blue background, or **bluescreen**.
- The giant mechanical shark, shown in Plate 2b. This element is a computer-generated image, built and rendered as a three-dimensional model completely within the computer.
- The water, shown in Plate 2c. The water element is also computer-generated 3D imagery.
- The sky, shown in Plate 2d. This element is a hand-painted backdrop (painted on canvas) that was photographed as a single frame.

Many other original elements make up this composite as well, most of them 3D elements. These include the reflections of the peach and the shark in the water, the smoke coming from the shark, shadows for the various elements, and spray and foam on the top of the water. Throughout the compositing process, additional elements may be generated that are the result of some manipulation performed on an original element. Plate 2e shows such an element: a specialized image known as a **matte** that is derived from the bluescreen peach element and that will be used to selectively add the peach into the scene.

As you can probably tell, most of the elements that we've shown have had some sort of additional processing performed on them as they were added into the final scene. Such processing, which might be used to modify the color of an image or the size of an element in the frame, is done throughout the compositing process in order to better integrate elements into their new environment.

You will commonly hear elements referred to as "layers," since the various elements are layered together to produce the eventual image. Original footage that is shot with a camera and transferred into a computer constitutes a subset of elements usually referred to as **plates**. Thus, the peach element in this example would be referred to as a plate. Typically, a synthetic image such as the water would *not* be termed a plate, nor would any intermediate elements that were generated during the process of creating a composite, such as the peach matte.

As you can see, there is little conceptual difference between the shot that was done for *King Kong* and recent composites such as that produced for *James and the Giant Peach*. The tools used may have evolved, but the intentions and basic methodology remain unchanged.

ORGANIZATION OF THE BOOK

This book will attempt to cover a range of topics related to digital compositing, from some basic concepts dealing with digital image acquisition and storage to specific aesthetic considerations necessary for producing a good composite. Initial chapters will provide enough background so that readers with only a basic knowledge of computers will find the book useful; in addition, there are a number of sections in this book that we hope even the most experienced professional will find useful.

The structure of a book such as this requires that the information be broken into well-defined categories. These categories (represented by chapters or sections within a chapter), while useful for organizational purposes, are ultimately somewhat arbitrary. The topics are all interrelated, and many discussions could easily have been placed into a number of different categories. To help identify related information, you will often find cross-references to relevant material that is located elsewhere in the book. The specific breakdown for how the chapters are organized is as follows:

- Chapter 2 presents an overview of how images are represented digitally, including some discussion about the process of converting images from other sources into a digital format.
- Chapter 3 covers some of the basic manipulations that are possible with digital images. These include using image processing tools that are designed to modify the color, size, and placement of elements within a scene.
- Chapter 4 takes this topic to the next step, with a look at the process of combining images or image sequences. This chapter is where the concept of a **matte**—an image that is used to selectively control certain combinatorial operations—is first introduced.
- Chapter 5 deals with these matte images in much greater detail—particularly with the methods that are commonly used to create and modify them.
- Chapter 6 is dedicated to concepts and techniques relating to imagery that changes over time, and to image manipulations that do the same.
- Chapter 7 looks at **tracking**, the process of analyzing and duplicating the motion of existing objects in a scene.
- Chapters 8 and 9 discuss a variety of methods that can be used to interact with the data, images, and software that you will be using.
- Chapter 10 is a broad overview of the various formats that might need to make use of digital compositing, from film to video to multimedia.
- Chapter 11 covers some important concepts that must be understood in order to work efficiently while still producing quality imagery—an area of great importance for any sizeable compositing projects.
- Chapter 12 describes characteristics of cameras and vision that must be understood in order to produce realistic, believable composites.
- Chapter 13 deals with some of the things that should happen *before* a composite is started, when the elements that will be used are being created.
- Chapter 14 rounds out a topic that we touch on throughout the book, namely, image and scene integration techniques, and gives some more specific suggestions.
- Finally, Chapter 15 goes into a bit more detail about certain topics that are of a more advanced nature and also touches on some disciplines that are related to compositing, such as digital painting and editing.
- The last chapter of the book, Chapter 16, uses all this preceding information to take an in-depth look at a number of well-known scenes that were created via the use of digital compositing. It should give a sense of how the topics that we've covered can be applied in real-world situations.

The book also includes a few appendices that deal with specific topics in greater detail.

- Appendix A provides a summary of the tools that should be part of a reasonably complete compositing package, extending the list of operators that are covered in the body of the book. This section should also prove useful if you need to evaluate the relative merits of competing pieces of software.
- Appendix B lists companies that provide digital compositing software, as well as software that is often used in conjunction with the compositing process.
- Appendix C attempts to list some of the popular file formats that are used to store digital images. This appendix also includes a more in-depth look at the Cineon file format, which is specifically designed for the representation of images that are shot on film.
- Appendix D documents some specific details about common film and video formats.

Although this book is primarily targeted at those who are actually creating digital composites, much of the information will also be important to individuals who need a more simplified overview of the subject. If this is the case, the following course of action is suggested.

1. In general, the introductory information at the beginning of each chapter gives a basic idea about what is contained in that chapter. If nothing else, read these introductions.

2. Chapter 2 defines a great deal of terminology. A basic understanding of the information contained in the section entitled "Image Generation" should be enough to make the rest of the book a bit more comprehensible.

3. Chapters 3 and 4 concentrate on specific tools, and as such may not be as relevant to someone who will not be involved with actual image creation. The section in Chapter 4 that discusses the concept of a matte is probably the only "must-read" section.

4. Chapters 5, 6, and 7 should be skimmed to get a basic idea of the concepts presented, but probably not much more than that is necessary. Chapters 8 and 9 are even less interesting to someone who will not be using any software directly.

5. Chapter 10 should probably only be looked at if there is a desire to understand a particular format in more detail. This may come up on a case-by-case basis.

6. Chapter 12 is important for anybody who wants to understand the visual nature of the compositing process. It is not terribly technical and should probably be read in its entirety. Chapter 13, on the other hand, will most likely be useful only if you are involved in the actual photography of the elements that will be used in a composite.

7. Chapter 15 is mostly composed of advanced topics, but the end of the chapter does touch on a few disciplines related to compositing that may be useful.

8. The final piece of the book, which may prove to be the most useful, is the glossary. Although it is not something that should be read from beginning to end in one sitting, it should prove to be a valuable resource as one encounters unfamiliar terms.

As you can probably see from some of these descriptions, the first part of this book tends to focus more on the *science* of digital compositing. We go over the basic technical concepts that one should become familiar with, and we describe the tools that are typically available. Once this technical foundation is laid, we then expand the focus to discuss more of the techniques, the *art*, behind the digital compositing process.

Whether or not you actually have any formalized artistic training should not deter you from learning the specific artistic skills that a good **compositor** (one who creates composites) uses on a daily basis. Part of this process involves learning the tools that are necessary. Just as a painter needs to understand the workings of pigments and canvas, a digital artist needs to have a technical understanding of the software involved. It is certainly possible to be an effective compositor without fully understanding all the technical issues that will be presented in this book. As with any other artistic discipline, experience and instinct can go a long way toward producing the final result. However, a basic understanding of the technology behind the tools can greatly improve the efficiency and problem-solving ability of even the best artists.

The rest of the art will come only with experience, although you will probably find that you are already well on your way. This is because you, and every other sighted person, have already spent a lifetime learning what reality looks like. The information may not always be consciously accessible, but the expert subconscious is surprisingly skilled at noticing when an image appears artificial or incorrect. This is both a blessing and a curse, since everyone else who will view your work will be similarly able to detect these problems. However, the ability to determine that there *is* a problem is the largest part of the process of realizing why the problem exists and learning how to fix it. Throughout this book we'll certainly try to point out the scenarios in which visual problems can arise. These problems will often involve well-defined **artifacts**—undesirable items in an image that are the result of the process used to create the image. But compositing problems can go far beyond specific identifiable glitches. Greater difficulties arise when trying to accurately duplicate the myriad of visual cues that would be present in a real image. These are the things that the subconscious is so much better at perceiving, and this is why someone who creates composite imagery must become an artist. The same knowledge that a painter uses—from the interaction of light and shadow to distance and perspective cues—will be necessary to create a believable digital composite.

There is one final piece of business to be dealt with before we can continue to the rest of the chapters in this book. A disclaimer:

> Different people, countries, and software packages do not always use the same names to refer to particular tools, operators, or subjects. In addition, due to the need to simplify certain things, just about every statement we make could probably be countered with some exception to the rule.

This statement isn't given in order to protect the author from any mistakes he's made within the pages of this book, but rather as a warning to anyone just starting to learn about this field. In many cases, you will find similar or identical concepts referred to by completely different names, depending on what book you are reading or to whom you are talking. Digital compositing is still a very young, volatile discipline. As such, there are many areas within it that have not become terribly well standardized.

A glossary is provided at the end of the book that attempts to cover a wide range of terms as they relate to digital compositing. Throughout the body of the text, terms being introduced are printed in bold to indicate that you will find a definition in the glossary. There are certainly places in the book where we have made some arbitrary decisions about a particular term and its usage. It is hoped this will help, rather than hinder, the process of terminology standardization within the industry.